FRANZ KAFKA

1. WHO WAS FRANZ KAFKA

Franz Kafka

Franz Kafka is classed as a famous Czech and international writer from the first half of the 20th century. He came from a German-Jewish family and wrote in German, but he also spoke and wrote very well in Czech. His whole life is associated with Prague's Old Town, although he occasionally moved outside its boundaries for a short while. Kafka loved Prague, but longed to free himself from it. He managed to temporarily do so with his last girlfriend, Dora Dymantová, when he moved to Berlin to live with her.

Franz Kafka was born on 3 July 1883 to Julie (Löwy) Kafková and Hermann Kafka, a merchant of haberdashery goods. The Kafka family had six children, however only the three younger sisters reached adulthood. Two brothers died early. Franz Kafka loved his family, but was not particularly close to them. Sometimes he spoke only a few words to his parents the entire day long, because there was not much to say. He fought with his emotional dependency on his family for a long time. But in spite of all the misunderstandings, it was virtually impossible for him to part with them. He tried to leave his family several times, but he eventually returned to them once he became seriously ill.

There were few people with whom he was actually close: his sister Ottla, Milena Jesenská, probably also his last love, Dora Dymantová and Max Brod.

Kafka finished elementary school on Masný trh (Meat Market). After completing his exams at the German State Grammar School in Old Town, he studied law at Charles-Ferdinand University in Prague. Afterwards, in 1907, he began working at the Italian insurance company Assicurazioni Generali and, one year later, at the Workmen's Accidental Insurance Company, where he remained until his early retirement in 1922.

Franz Kafka wanted to marry several times, but he was scared of the intimacy of a relationship and how it could possibly affect his writing. Marriage would certainly hinder his literary work, as was the case with his job. Still he longed to love and belong to someone. He did not want to be alone, but also needed to be.

His approach to his writing was equally ambivalent. Writing was his life, but he did not like to present it to anyone. His was unsure about its publication. He was very critical of his own writing. The immortal story about Kafka's unfulfilled wish that his friend Max Brod destroy his works after his death confirms our conception of the contradictory Kafka who loved his works and their creation, but instead insisted upon their destruction.

Beneath the surface of this reality, we see Kafka as a very sensitive person who longed for appreciation from his loved ones, including his father and even himself.

His friend Max Brod discovered the quality of Kafka's personality and his work as a Czech writer during Kafka's lifetime. They had met in 1902 whilst studying and Brod had introduced Kafka to the literary Prague-German environment. Although Kafka's personality was completely different from Brod's, they understood each other well from the literary and human point of view. Brod was active and socially successful, whereas Kafka avoided social life. Brod was a passionate Zionist, whereas Kafka did not perceive his religion through politics. He began to learn Hebrew and was interested in the Yiddish theatre, which he himself supported. He was

F.K. is regarded as one of the greatest writers in the world.

fascinated by its harsh atmosphere and strength of speech, as forms of expression that he was encountering for the first time in his life.

The personality and works of Franz Kafka were later intentionally ignored during the Nazi and Communist regime. André Breton and the surrealistic circle of the review entitled *Minotaur* were the new discovers of Kafka's work.

Another significant point, radically changing the course of Kafka's life, was his incurable illness. On the night of 12 and 13 August 1917, Kafka suffered his first attack of vomiting up blood. In September, the doctor surmised that he had lung tuberculosis. Kafka refused treatment at a clinic where he was sent by his family and friends. He preferred to see his beloved sister Ottla at the farm in Siřem.

In Franz Kafka's life and in his person, we can, in many ways, sense a form of instability. However, there is a simultaneous longing for balance, accompanied by an inability to obtain it or maintain it. Within his family relationships, the institution of marriage and family life, his job and bond with his native Prague, as well as his literary work, there is a polarity of emotions and opinions. There is a longing for the realisation of his wishes at times when everything was already doomed to failure.

Kafka's work consists of prose stories, three unfinished novels, diaries, traveller's diaries and correspondence.

During his life Franz Kafka agreed to the publication of only a few of his works. After his death Max Brod arranged and edited his works. He began publishing them in the Mercy Publishing House in Prague and in the Schocken Publishing House in Berlin. Brod collected most of the works from the Kafka family and Milena Jesenská. During his own life, Brod came into possession of several of Kafka's works. The only things missing were the letters to Felice Bauer and the letters to the family that the Kafka family decided to keep, in addition to the "Letter to His Father" and *The Metamorphosis*. He did not have the manuscripts from the previous years that Kafka had dedicated to Dora Dymantová; they had gone missing in 1933 during a search of her flat by the Gestapo. The relatives of Milena Jesenská kept the letters addressed to her.

Brod took most of the manuscripts to Palestine, where he emigrated. In 1961 he presented them to the niece of Franz Kafka.

In the 1960's, Professor Eduard Goldstücker attempted a literary and social rehabilitation of Kafka and his works. He regarded them as something that was discovered in a new manner by each young generation. Even today, Kafka's influence remains. It is timeless and presents a world in which the old forms of security no longer apply, whilst faith in human progress is stagnating. The individual retreats to a secluded place, where there is a feeling of guilt and a need to engage in a new world, to find peace and order.

Max Brod, the friend and propagator of F.K.

2. THE LIFE OF FRANZ KAFKA IN DATES

1883 Franz Kafka was born on 3 July in Prague as the firstborn son of Julia, (1856-1934) and Hermann Kafka (1852-1931) in the house known as "U věže" ("At the Tower") on the corner of Kaprova and Maiselova Streets (today called "Náměstí Franze Kafky" [Franz Kafka Square]).

1885-1888 During these years the Kafka family lived in many parts of Prague: 56 Wenceslas Square, 5 Dušní Street and 6 Mikulášská Street (later demolished).

1885 The Kafka family had a second son, Georg, who died of measles in 1887.
1887 A third son, Heinrich was born, who died after a six-month ear infection.

1888-1889 The Kafka family lived at 2 Celetná Street.

1889-1892 The family lived in the house called "U minuty" (At the Minute) at 2/3 Old Town Square. All three sisters of Franz Kafka were born here.

1889-1893 Kafka attended primary school on "Masný trh" ("Meat Market") (today "Masná ulice" [Meat Street]).

1889 Sister Elli (Gabriele) was born.

1890 Sister Valli (Valerie) was born.

1892 Sister Ottla (Ottilie) was born.

1892-1907 The Kafka family lived at 3 Celetná, in the house called "U Tří králů" ("At the Three Kings").

1893-1901 Kafka attended the German State Grammar School on Old Town Square in the Kinský Palace. Franz Kafka makes friends with Oskar Pollak.

1896 Bar mitzvah in the Cikánská synagoga (Gipsy Synagogue) (later demolished).

1899-1903 First experiments in literature (later destroyed). Kafka read Nietzsche and Spinoza.

The parents and the family house in Prague's Old Town Quarter

1901-1906 Kafka began reading chemistry (for two weeks only) and German literature, but switched to reading law at Charles-Ferdinand University in Prague. He spent his holidays with his uncle Siegfried Löwy, a doctor in Třešť, Moravia.

1902 He met Max Brod, a classmate who was a year younger – writer, critic and editor of the *Prager Tagblatt* and the blind writer Oskar Baum.

1903 He wrote the novel *Dítě a město (The Child and the City)* (which has since gone missing).

1903-1904 He developed "Reflections for Gentlemen-Jockeys."
He read the letters of Goethe, Dubarry, as well the biographies of Schopenhauer and Dostoevsky.

1905 He spent the summer in a treatment clinic in Zuckmantel in Silesia, where he fell passionately in love with an unknown older woman.

1906 He was employed in Dr. Richard Löwy's law firm in Prague. In June he was awarded a PhD in law. As of October he was practicing law at court.
The following short stories were developed: "The Trees," "Excursion into the Mountains," "The Street Window," "Children on a Country Road" and "The Refusal" (later included in the anthology called *Looking to Sea*).

1907-1913 The family moved to 36/883 Mikulášská Street (today Pařížská Street), into the house called "U lodi" ("At the Ship"), which was later demolished (the Hotel Intercontinental stands here today).

1907-1908 He wrote "Svatební přípravy na venkově" ("Preparations for a Marriage in the Countryside: A Fragment").

1907 He was employed in the Prague branch of the Italian insurance company Assicurazioni Generali.

1908 He began working as a lawyer for the Workmen's Accident Insurance Company. He worked there until 1920 when he was forced to leave his employment due to illness.
His friendship with Max Brod deepened; they travelled together to Riva and Brescia.
He published eight parts of the collection later known as *Meditation* in the Munich literary magazine *Hyperion*.

1909 The Prague German newspaper *Bohemia* printed Kafka's "Aeroplanes in Brescia."

The cook used to take small Franz to school across Old Town Square.

He became a member of the intellectual circle that met at Berta Fantová's home, in the house "U jednorožce" ("At the Unicorn") at 17 Old Town Square. Many famous people visited this salon, including Albert Einstein during his stay in Prague.

In summer he left with Max Brod for Paris. They planned to write the novel *Richard and Samuel* together.

He began writing his travel diaries.

1910   In May, he began writing a diary in which he wrote his last entry on 12th June 1923. In October he left with Max and Otto Brod for Paris; he came back alone due to his illness. In December he travelled to Berlin.

1911   He spent his holidays with Max Brod in northern Italy. On their journey they travelled through Munich, Zurich, Lucerne, Lugano, Milan as far as Lago Maggiore. From here they continued to Paris and then back to Milan.

For the first time, Kafka visited a performance of the Yiddish theatre in the Café Savoy and began taking a deeper interest in it. He made friends with Jicchak Löwy, the main actor of the theatre group and with other Hassidic actors from Galicia.

Kafka's father convinced him to set up an asbestos factory. He participated in this project with his brother-in-law Karl Hermann and it lasted until 1917, without major success.

Kafka began writing the novel *The One Who Went Missing (America)*.

1912   He began to study Judaism. In February he lectured on the Yiddish language in the Jewish municipal house on Maiselova Street, where he also organised a benefit performance for Jicchak Löwy's theatre group.

In July he left with Max Brod for Weimar and then stayed alone at a treatment clinic in Harz.

He met with the publishers Ernst Rowohlt and Kurt Wolff.

On 13 August Kafka met the assistant of a Berlin trading company, Felice Bauer, in the house of Max Brod's father on Skořepka Street. In October he began his correspondence with her under the excuse of a planned journey to Palestine.

During the night from 22 to 23 September between 10 p.m. and 6 a.m., he wrote "The Judgement." He dedicated it to Felice.

In September and October he wrote the chapter "The Stoker" that later became a part of his unfinished novel *The One Who Went Missing or America*, the name given to the novel by Max Brod.

From October 1912 until February 1913, he wrote no diary entries. However, his correspondence with Felice further developed. He wrote up to four letters a day to her.

In November and December he wrote *The Metamorphosis*.

1913 Rowohlt published *Meditation* in Leipzig. In spring "The Judgement" and "The Stoker" were published.
He visited Felice Bauer's family twice in Berlin.
He travelled to Vienna, Venice, and Riva on the shores of Lago di Garda, where he experienced a romantic affair with a Swiss girl lasting the ten days of his stay.

1913-1914 He lived in Oppelt's house with his parents on the corner of Old Town Square and Pařížská Street.

1914 In spring Kafka got engaged to Felice Bauer, but in July he broke off the engagement. He began to exchange letters with a close friend of Felice Bauer's, Grete Bloch, who acted as their go-between at the time of their separation.
In February, Kafka moved away from his parents' lodging into various rented flats (to make room for his sisters who came to live at their parents' home with their children for part of the war): 10 Bílkova Street, then to 16 Dlouhá "U Zlaté štiky" (At the Golden Pike) and finally to 48 Polská Street in Vinohrady. His sisters' husbands were on the front. Kafka was excused from military service.
He travels to the Baltic Sea with his friend Ernst Weiss.
In autumn he begins writing *The Trial*.

1915 At the start of the year he renewed his relationship with Felice.
He continued work on *The Trial*. In November Rowohlt published *The Metamorphosis* in Leipzig. He received money after being awarded the Fontane literary prize for *The Metamorphosis*, *Meditation* and "The Stoker."
In December 1915 and in January 1916 he wrote "The Village Schoolmaster (The Giant Mole)," "Blumfeld, an elderly Bachelor." He also wrote *In the Penal Colony*, "Before the Law" and "A Dream."
He travelled to Hungary with his sister Elli.

1916 In July Kafka met with Felice Bauer in Mariánské lázně.
In August he made a list of positive and negative factors of marriage.
He worked on stories that were later assembled in "A Country Doctor."
In this period he occasionally spent time at 22 Zlatá ulička, where he slept at his sister Ottla's home. The following prose works were created here: "The Hunter Gracchus," "The Bucket Rider," "The Great Wall of China," "My Neighbour," "A Crossbreed (A Sport)" and "The Bridge."
He gave a reading from his prose work *In the Penal Colony* at Goltz's bookshop in Munich.

F. K. was employed as a lawyer at the Workmen's Accidental Insurance Company in Prague.

1917 He moved into the Schönbornský Palace on Tržiště Street (today the building housing the American Embassy).
He began to learn Hebrew.
In July he got engaged in Prague to Felice Bauer for the second time.
In August the first signs of his illness appeared, he vomited up blood and in September he was diagnosed with tuberculosis.
He went to the farm at Siřem to see his sister Ottla. In December he stopped working and writing in his diary.
He broke off the engagement to Felice.
He created a collection of aphoristic texts, stories and fragments, the so-called "Siřemské zápisky" ("The Siřem Entries").

1918-1924 He occasionally spent time in Oppelt's house with his parents.

1918 From the start of the year until April he stayed in Siřem. The following prose works were created here: "A Common Confusion," "The Truth about Sancho Panza," "The Silence of the Sirens," "Prometheus."
He continued writing aphorisms, which Max Brod later named "Úvahy o hříchu, utrpení, naději a pravé cestě" ("Reflections on Sin, Pain, Hope and the True Way").
From May he again shortly worked for the Workmen's Accident Insurance Company.
In October he contracted Spanish flu.
At the end of the year he left for Želízy u Liběchova nad Labem (Schelesen), where he lived in Studlov's hostel for convalescing patients. There he met Julia Wohryzková, the daughter of the caretaker of the synagogue in Vinohrady, who was also there for rehabilitation.

1920 In spring he lived in Prague. At the time when Felice Bauer got married, Franz Kafka became engaged to Julia Wohryzková. In November he withdrew his offer of marriage.
Kafka spent the winter with Max Brod in Želízy.
"A Country Doctor" and *In the Penal Colony* were published.
In November he wrote "Letter to His Father."

1921 From January 1920 until October 1921, he did not make any diary entries.
Terminally ill, he ended his work at the Workmen's Accidental Insurance Company.
From April until June he lived in Merano, and during the latter half of the year, in Prague.
He wrote a series of stories: "He," "At Night," "The City Coat of Arms," "Fellowship," "Rejection," "The Problem of Our Laws," "The Test," "A Little Fable," "The Vulture."
In 1921-1924 he wrote stories that were later compiled in "A Hunger Artist."

New works were often inspired by long night walks through Prague.

He met the writer Milena Jesenská, who at the time lived in Vienna with her husband Oskar Pollak. Their correspondence began.

In December he went to the treatment clinic in Matliary in the Tatra Mountains. He made friends with Robert Klopstock, a student of medicine, who, like Kafka, was also being treated at the clinic.

In his diaries, Kafka doubts that he will be able to find the meaning of life.

Kafka gave his diaries to Milena Jesenská. He remained at the treatment clinic in the Tatra Mountains, later in September he returned to Prague.

1922 Kafka began writing *The Castle*; later he decided not to complete it. He also created "The Investigations of a Dog."

He met Milena Jesenská for the last time.

In January and February, he lived in the town of Špindlerův Mlýn and then returned to Prague. Over the summer he stayed with Ottla in Planá nad Lužnicí in a summer flat.

1923 Kafka spent July with his sister Elli in a summer camp organized by the Jewish home in Muritz on the Baltic Sea, where he met a young Zionist, Dora Dymantová, who came from a Polish Orthodox Jewish family.

At the end of September he left with Dora for Berlin, where they lived in Miquelstrasse and later in Grunewaldstrasse.

He attended lectures on Jewish studies at the Berlin Academy.

He wrote "Doupě" ("The Burrow"). He sent "A Hunger Artist" to the publishers.

1924 He wrote "Josephine the Singer, or the Mouse Folk."

Terminally ill, he was transported by Max Brod from Berlin to Prague, where he lived with his parents in Oppelt's house for about fourteen days.

In April he left for the Weiner Wald treatment clinic and then moved to the clinic in Kierling near Vienna. It was Dora Dymantová and Robert Klopstock who brought him there.

Franz Kafka died here on 3 June.

The funeral took place on 11 June in the New Jewish Cemetery in Strašnice.

In summer "A Hunger Artist" was published.

Dora Dymantová, the treatment clinic in Kierling and the gravestone of F.K. in Prague

3. THE FAMILY AND FRIENDS OF FRANZ KAFKA

Hermann Kafka and Julia Kafková, the parents of Franz Kafka

The father of Franz Kafka came from the village Osek in Southern Bohemia. He was the son of Jakob Kafka, a shocheta (a ritual butcher), and of Franzsiska Platowská. He was born in modest circumstances, but worked his way to becoming a successful merchant of haberdashery goods in Prague. His shop was situated on Old Town Square in the Kinský Palace.

Kafka's mother, Julie Kafková, was born in Poděbrady in 1856. She came from a rich and educated family of rabbis, scholars and mystics. The core of Kafka's talents presumably originates from here. The father Herman's relatives were not as religious.

Kafka's favourite uncle, Siegfried Löwy, came from the mother's side of the family. He was a humorous, old bachelor and a doctor in Třešt, where Franz Kafka spent his school holidays.

Julie Kafková also gave her first-born son Franz the Hebrew name Amschel, after her grandfather who she remembered as a well-respected man studying the Talmud and abandoning his trade.

The relationship of Hermann with his son is one of the focal points that shaped the personality and work of Franz Kafka. The pragmatically thinking father – the businessman – and the son – the intellectual thinker – had a complicated relationship with mutual misunderstandings and disagreements about existence. The father often reminisced concerning his own childhood and youth, full of privations and hard work, and thereby placed constant pressure on Franz. According to his father, Franz's choice for marriage or a solid work placement were supposed to help him achieve status in life, however Kafka felt the opposite. He wished to concentrate solely on writing, which he considered sufficient for fulfilling his goals in life. This dichotomy suggests that Hermann Kafka was neither able to appreciate his son's literary activity, nor approach Franz in a human manner. The priorities of father and son were too far apart.

The painful autobiographic document "Letter to His Father" was inspired by the unequal relationship between father and son. This document is considered, even with regard to the circumstances and the period when it was written, as over-exaggerated and as partially distorting their actual relationship. Kafka talks to his father about his expectations and opinions. He feels sorry that his father did not guide him more strictly towards religion. He lists the ways in which he believes that he disappointed his father. This was the first time that he openly, even if in literary form, was able to express his disagreement. The letter was never delivered. His mother Julie refused to give it to his father. The question remains whether this letter would have changed anything or only contributed to a deeper estrangement.

Ottla Kafková, the youngest sister of Franz Kafka

Ottla was Kafka's favourite member of the family and his closest confidante, next to his friend, Max Brod. She understood her brother's relationship with their father and often felt the deep differences between her own opinions versus those of her father.

Kafka's close relationship with Ottla was proven when he went to see her at Siřem in 1917 after his diagnosis was confirmed and his engagement to Felice had been broken off. She was working in Siřem on the farm of her brother-in-law, Karl Hermann, the husband of her sister Elli.

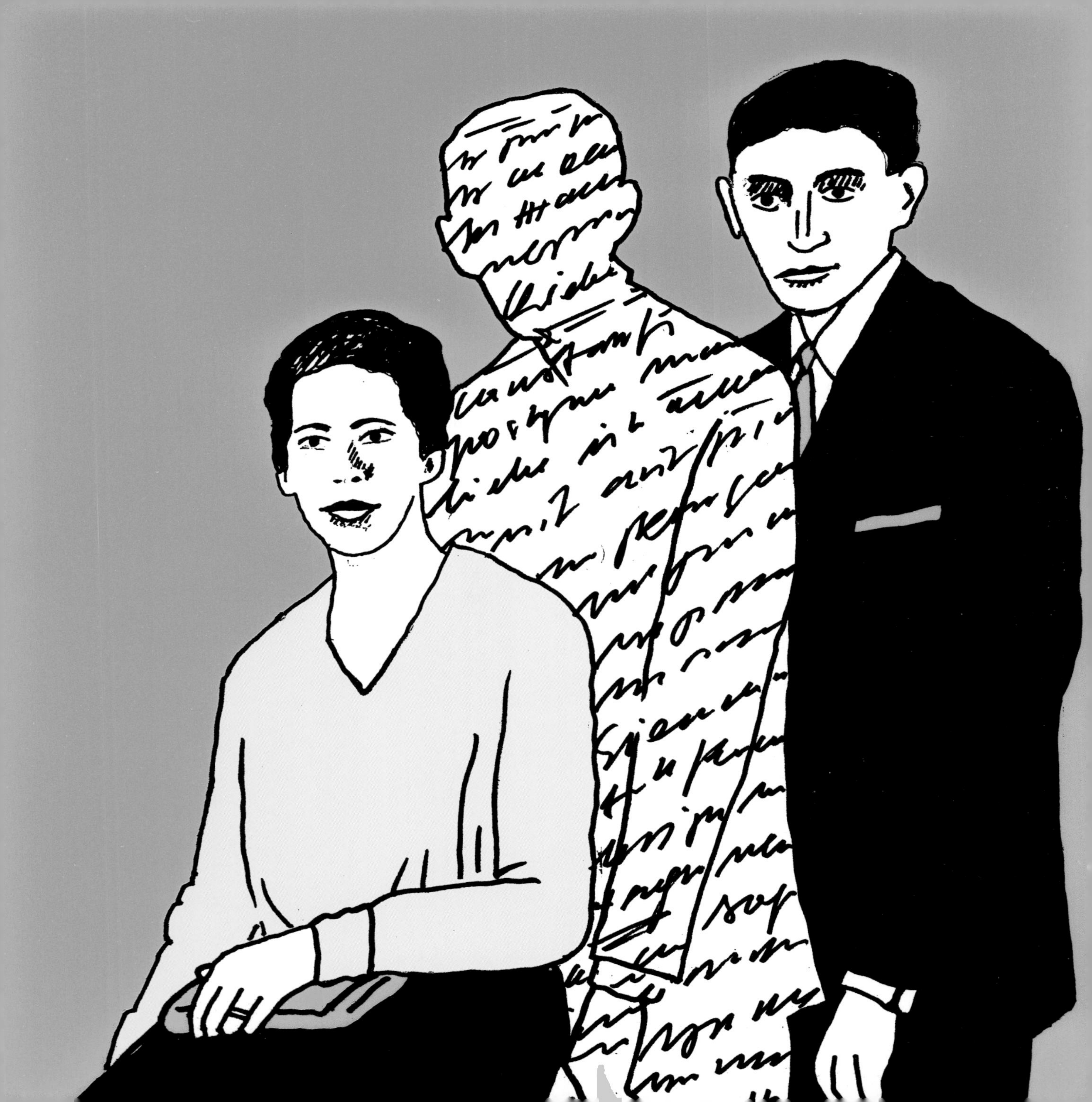

The twenty-five-year-old and single Ottla had accepted Hermann's offer and left her father's shop to work on the farm in Siřem. She was interested in agriculture. Morever, the Hermann family was one of the wealthiest families in Siřem. They owned vast plots of land and thus Ottla had the best prospects for work and self-fulfilment.

For Kafka, the isolated stay in Siřem was a struggle for independence, a balancing of his own life, as well as a test of his ability to live outside his family's influence. Ottla was constantly at his side during this time.

Kafka was full of praise for his sister. He valued her ability to listen, her kindness and the independence with which she would eventually choose her own husband. The other sisters, Valli and Elli, married in accordance to their father's wishes.

The life of his beloved sister Ottla had a tragic end in 1942 in Osvětim, where, of her own freewill, she accompanied a transport of Jewish children from Terezín. Elli and Valli, as well as their families, shared the same fate. Apparently they disappeared in concentration camps or in a Lodz ghetto.

Felice Bauer, Franz Kafka's girlfriend

In 1913 Kafka met Felice Bauer, who was from Berlin, at his friend, Max Brod's house. In his diaries, he mentions that Felice fascinated him at first sight. Shortly afterwards a lively correspondence began between them. Franz visited Felice in Berlin and later met her family with her own income.

For her times, Felice was a highly innovative and independent woman. She had worked up from the assistant of a firm to becoming a company-secretary. At the time of the financial crisis, she supported her family with her won income.

When Kafka was considering his engagement to Felice and was waiting for the consent of her father to the marriage, he expressed his characteristic and repetitive doubts concerning the nature of married life and his part within it in his diaries. He writes that he is unable to remain in a marriage or a family and that his employment bores him. His only fulfilment in life is literature and not even marriage will change that. It appears that he forgot other positive aspects of life.

The practical Felice shared the views of Franz's parents, she longed for a peaceful and secure life. Kafka must have sensed this. Kafka proved his inability to handle marriage and its responsibilities by twice breaking off the engagement to Felice within a considerably short time. The diagnosis of his illness prompted their second parting, and in doing so, he relieved himself of the responsibility of fulfilling the promise that he doubted he could honour.

Julie Wohryzková, the second fiancée of Franz Kafka

In 1918, Kafka met Julia Wohryzková, the daughter of a shoemaker and a servant at the Vinohrady synagogue, in Želízy, where they were both convalescing.

Their engagement in 1919 lasted only a short time. For Kafka, it was another hopeless attempt at a well-arranged family lifestyle and at the achievement of demands naturally expected of him.

Although he had a good relationship with Julia, this would have been a marriage of convenience. Self-doubt soon prevailed. He realised how hopeless the situation was. It was impossible for a young, healthy girl to live a married life with a seriously ill and unsettled man.

Given the social impropriety of the marriage, Kafka's father Hermann could not agree with his son's choice of wife. This led to the "Letter to His Father" which was thus based on the lifelong tension between father and son, as well as their argument over Julia Wohryzková.

Literature proved to be an impediment in Kafka's relation to women.

Milena Jesenská, Kafka's close friend and the first translator of Kafka's works into Czech

Milena Jesenská was born in 1896 in Prague to a family, where the father was a professor of medicine at Charles University. This was the same year of Franz Kafka's Bar mitzvah and he later claimed that she was a gift to his maturity.

Milena's mother, with whom she had a close relationship, died when Milena was sixteen, and she never got on with her strict father. She studied at the girl's academy Minerva, where progressive feminist views were beginning to develop.

When she was twenty, she met Ernst Pollak, a bank clerk ten years her senior, who preferred to devote himself to literature, art and political discussions in Prague cafés, where Franz Kafka, Max Brod, Franz Werfel and others met. Franz and Milena must have met during that time, but Kafka did not remember her from that period.

After a long and tragically culminating argument with her anti-Semitic minded father, Milena married Pollak and moved to Vienna with him. She gradually improved her German and became engaged in literary work.

In 1919 she encountered the interesting story of "The Stoker" by a not-particularly-famous Prague writer, Franz Kafka. She wrote, informing him that she would like to translate it into Czech. This was when their correspondence began and it lasted until 1923. During the years 1920-1923, she translated "The Stoker," six prose texts from the collection *Meditation* and "A Report to an Academy" from the cycle "A Country Doctor" and "The Judgement."

The relationship of Milena and Franz took place primarily though letters. They only met a few times in person. This partnership did not have a future. At the time Milena was unable to leave Pollak and Franz had only just broken off his engagement to Felice. In addition to his, he was concerned about having an intimate relationship. He was extremely sensitive and also seriously ill with an ever-diminishing belief in his own recovery.

The intensity of his relationship with Milena was confirmed in 1922 when Kafka dedicated all his diaries to her. Even after their separation he read her articles and bought newspapers in which they were published.

After Kafka's death, Milena decided to leave her husband and left for Prague where she worked as a writer and journalist. After the German invasion of Bohemia in 1939, she actively participated in illegal movements trying to help prominent Czechs and Jews escape from the country. However, she was too friendly and naive, and thus she was also soon arrested. In 1940 she was sent to Ravensbruck concentration camp in Germany. Other prisoners admired her for her firm convictions. In 1944 she died of a serious illness, she was 47 years old.

In 1995 she was awarded the title "Spravedlivý mezi národy" ("The Righteous Amongst the Nations") at the Yad Vashem Memorial for her attempts at saving Czech Jews during the war.

Dora Dymantová, the last girlfriend of Franz Kafka

Dora Diamantová, who later changed her name to Dymantová, was born in Poland into a Jewish-Orthodox family. She was, however, fascinated by the western world and its culture and thus moved to Germany. After an unsuccessful attempt by her father to bring her home, she remained in Berlin. Her father never despised her for this, as she always visited her home and observed the family traditions.

Dora and Franz Kafka met in Müritz on the Baltic Sea, in a summer colony organized by the Jewish home, where Franz had come to visit his sister Elli. Later on in 1923, Kafka went to Berlin to see Dora and together, they rented a flat there.

At the beginning, they were a happy couple. Franz could finally leave his home, as well as his beloved, but also hated Prague. He was now living his own life in a city which he loved. It seems that he had enough peace for his work, but later

forced Dora to destroy some of the stories that he had written there. In the modest conditions of Berlin life, Franz Kafka's state of health quickly deteriorated. By 1924 he was unable to speak or move and Max Brod took him to Prague. Dora later accompanied him to the Kierling treatment clinic where he died shortly thereafter.

Their short relationship was probably very intensive, enhanced by the difficult circumstances in which they were living. Both felt lonely, although intimate when together. They focused on their planned departure for Palestine. Whilst working, Kafka liked to have Dora next to him and in the evening he read aloud what he wrote during the day.

They were very poor, however, the seriously-ill Kafka, who only had a few months left to live, felt free and happy because he was able to do what he had tried in vain to achieve all his life – to separate himself from his family and become independent. He refused visits from his parents, but always welcomed his sister and friends.

However, once his condition worsened, he returned to Prague. The doctors immediately sent him to a clinic for treatment. Dora followed him there and met Kafka's friend Dr. Klopstock.

It was Kafka's wish, that upon his death, Klopstock should take Dora away, so she would not see him dying. Instead, Kafka called Dora back at the fateful moment. She returned with a bunch of flowers that she had picked for him and stayed with Kafka. After the death of Kafka, Dr. Klopstock wrote a letter to the Kafka family. One of the sentences said: "Only the person who knows Dora knows what love is." Dora's first meeting with the parents of Franz Kafka was at his funeral in Prague. Their meeting was not warm. Dora later finished acting school. Franz Kafka had supported her in this. She got married and named her daughter Franziska. Dora became a successful actress of the Yiddish theatre and also became a writer for the Yiddish newspaper. The dream she dreamt of with Kafka during their time in Berlin came true. She visited Israel, where she met with her brother and sister, the only relatives left who survived the holocaust.

Max Brod

Max Brod met his best friend Franz Kafka for the first time in 1902 at the Prague-German University student society.

He was born in 1884 in Prague into a Jewish family. Similarly to Kafka, he had Czech citizenship, wrote in German, was a writer and a journalist. Not only was he Kafka's closest friend, but he was also the editor of his works that were partly, thanks to Max Brod, saved and published after Kafka's death. Brod and Kafka both studied at Charles-Ferdinand University in Prague. As of 1912 he was an active Zionist and he passed these views on to Kafka. Kafka was never over-active politically; even though he showed a lively interest in politics, he did not want to be engaged in these matters. In 1939 Max Brod immigrated to Palestine to escape the Nazi regime. In Israel, he was employed in writing and worked for the theatre.

He was a close friend and colleague of Kafka's. They shared their written pieces and read them aloud to one another. Kafka was very shy and he did not like showing his work to other people. Brod was thus one of the few friends to whom Kafka entrusted his work. This is confirmed by Kafka's wish that Brod destroy his work after his death. In the end, Brod did not fulfil Kafka's wishes and thereby saved the hitherto unpublished work that he himself eventually edited for publishing in 1930.

Brod's biography of Franz Kafka raised much interest and displayed great insight into the character of his friend and their relationship. Brod also edited Kafka's diaries and correspondence.

In his book *Český kruh (The Czech Circle)* about Czech literature in the first half of the 20th Century, Brod characterises and ranks writers of the Prague milieu into several groups. He felt closest to his friends Franz Kafka, Oskar Baum or Felix Weltsch and dubs this group "Český kruh" ("The Czech Circle").

The intellectual circle at 17 Staroměstské náměstí: Werfel, Rilke, Kisch, Kafka, Meyrink, Brod, Hašek, Einstein

4. FRANZ KAFKA AND PRAGUE

Residences:

- ❶ 5 Náměstí Franze Kafky
- ❷ 2 Malé náměstí
- ❸ 2 Celetná
- ❹ 3 Celetná
- ❺ 36 Mikulášská (today Pařížská)
- ❻ 5 Staroměstské náměstí
- ❼ 10 Bílkova
- ❽ 16 Dlouhá
- ❾ 22 Zlatá ulička

Education:

- ❿ 16 Masná (German Elementary School)
- ⓫ 12 Staroměstské náměstí (State German Grammar School)
- ⓬ 9 Železná (Charles University)

Employment:

- ⓭ 19 Václavské náměstí (Assicurazioni Generali Insurance Company)
- ⓮ 7 Na Poříčí (Workmen's Accidental Insurance Company)

5. THE WORKS OF FRANZ KAFKA

- Reflections for Gentlemen-Jockeys: A Fragment" (1904)
- "Wedding Preparations in the Country: A Fragment" (1907)
- *Meditation* (1908 - 1912, book edition 1913, 1915)
- "The Stoker" (1912, book edition 1913, 1916, 1918)
- "The Metamorphosis" (1912, journal edition 1915, book edition 1916, 1918)
- *The One Who Went Missing / America* (1912 - 1914, book edition 1927, critical edition in 2 vol. 1990)
- *The Trial* (1914 - 1915, book edition 1925, critical edition in 2 vol. 1983)
- In the Penal Colony (1914, book edition 1919)
- "A Country Doctor" (1915 - 1919, book edition 1919)
- "Letter to His Father" (manuscript 1919, edition 1952)
- *The Castle* (1922, book edition 1926, critical edition in 2 vol. 1982)
- "A Hunger Artist" (1922 - 1924, book edition 1924)
- *Stories* (1909-1924, book edition 1935)
- "Reflections for Gentlemen-Jockeys" (1909 - 1924, book edition 1936, 1954)
- *Wedding Preparations in the Country and Other Prose from the Estate* (1907-1919, book edition 1953)
- *Pamphlets and Fragments from the Estate I* (critical edition in 2 vol. 1992)
- *Pamphlets and Fragments from the Estate II* (critical edition in 2 vol. 1993)
- Works published during his lifetime (critical edition in 2 vol. 1996)
- *Diaries* (book edition 1937 - an anthology)
- *Diaries* (1909 - 1923, book edition 1951, critical edition in 3 vol. 1990)
- *Letters to Milena* (1920 - 1923, book edition 1952, extended edition 1983)
- *Letters to Family, Friends and Editors* (1958)
- *Letters to Felice* (1967)
- *Letters to Ottla and the Family* (1974)
- *Letters to Parents* 1922/1924 (1990)

Books printed in Czech:

- *Starý list* (An Old Manuscript) (1928)
- *Sen (A Dream)* (1929)
- *Zpráva pro akademii* (A Report to an Academy) (1929)
- *Proměna (The Metamorphosis)* (1929, 1963, 1990)
- *Venkovský lékař (A Country Doctor)* (1931)
- *Zámek (The Castle)* (1935, new translation 1969, 1989, 1997)
- *Pozorování (Contemplation* - an anthology 1946)
- *Proces (The Trial)* (1958, 1965, 1992, 1995, new translation 1997)
- *America (America)* (1962, a new translation under the title Missing 1990)
- *Povídky (Stories)* (1964, 1983, 1990)
- *Popis jednoho zápasu (Reflections for Gentlemen-Jockeys)* (1968, 1991, 1996)
- *Dopisy Mileně (Letters to Milena)* (1968, extended version 1993)
- *Aforismy (Aphorisms)* (1968, 1991)
- *Dopisy Felice (Letters to Felice* - an anthology 1991)
- *Obří krtek (The Giant Mole)* (1991)
- *Dopisy Ottle a rodině (Letters to Ottla and the Family)* (1996)
- *Dopisy otci a jiné nepublikované prózy (Letters to Father and Other unpublished prose)* (1996)
- *Deníky I (Diaries I)* (1909 - 1912) (1997)
- *Deníky II (Diaries II)* (1913 - 1923) (1998)
- *Franz Kafka - Max Brod, Přátelství* (Korespondence) (*Franz Kafka - Max Brod, Friendship*) (Correspondence) (1998)

Name:	Franz Kafka
Date of birth:	3 July 1883
Place of birth:	Prague, Bohemia
Parents:	Julie Löwy Kafková (1856 - 1934), Hermann Kafka (1852 - 1931)
Siblings:	Georg (1885-1886), Heinrich (1887 - 1888) Gabriele „Elli" (1889 - 1942?), Valerie „Valli" (1890-1942?), Ottilie „Ottla" (1892 - 1942)
Citizenship:	Austria-Hungary, from 1918 the Czechoslovak Republic
Religion:	Jewish
Education:	PhD in Law, Charles-Ferdinand University in Prague, awarded degree in 1906
Employment:	Employed as a lawyer at an insurance company
Height:	1.82 m
Weight:	between 65 - 45 kg (fluctuated due to illness)
Eye colour:	grey-blue
Hair colour:	black
Death:	3 June 1924, treatment clinic in Kierling near Vienna, Austria
Diagnosis at death:	tuberculosis
Age:	40 years and 11 months

Selected works:

Bergerová, Natalie. *Na křižovatce kultur/Historie Československých Židů*. Praha 1992.

Brod, Max. *Franz Kafka*. Praha 2000.

Canetti, Elias. *Der andere Prozeß: Kafkas Briefe an Felice*. München 1969.

Čermák, Karel and Juan Fleming. *Pražské vademecum Franze Kafky*. Praha 2004.

Franz Kafka: *Vzpomínky současníků*. Praha 2004.

Glatzer, Nahum Norbert. *The Loves of Franz Kafka*. New York 1986.

Heller, Erich. *The Basic Kafka*. New York, 1976.

Mailloux, Peter. *A Hesitation before Birth: the Life of Franz Kafka*. Newark 1989.

Northey, Anthony. *Kafka's Relatives: Their Lives and His Writing*. New Haven 1991.

The City of Kafka (Franz Kafka and Prague), catalogue of the exhibition in the Centre de Cultura Contemporania de Barcelona. Barcelona 2002.

Wagenbach, Klaus. *Franz Kafka*. Praha 1967 (2. ed.1993).

Franz Kafka – The Life and Works of a Prague Writer
Assembled by Marína Votrubová
Illustrations and graphic design by Jiří Votruba
Translation into English from Czech: Clarice Cloutier
Typography DTP and print TRIA
Published by Fun Explosive Praha 2005, 1st Edition
Hošťálkova 2,Praha 6
www.funexplosive.cz, www.votruba.cz

We thank the society of Franz Kafka of Prague for their help